End Writer's Block

By Amanda Symonds

This short book was designed to be read in one sitting so that the reader could identify where they are getting stuck and try a couple of methods to overcome their problem and produce some work that gets them out of their rut. You will get the maximum benefit if you can take action directly after reading the book and before life gets in the way of your writing again!

Copyright © Amanda Symonds 2022

Contents

What is Writer's Block?	5
Is Writer's Block Real?	6
Quotes with Advice From Famous Writers	7
Summary Tips to End Writer's Block	13
Writing Techniques	15
How Persistence in Writing Helps Overcome Writer's Block	18
How Lowering Your Expectations Helps Overcome Writer's Block	20
How Reading Books when Writing Helps Overcome Writer's Block	22
How Brainstorming when Writing Helps Overcome Writer's Block	23
How Stopping When You Are Ahead Helps Overcome Writer's Block	25
How Having a Change of Scene Helps Overcome Writer's Block	26
How Taking Regular Breaks Helps Overcome Writer's Block	28
How Keeping a Writing Journal Helps Overcome Writer's Block	30
How Starting at the End Helps Overcome Writer's Block	31
How Using Software Helps Overcome Writer's Block	33
How Writing Exercises Help Overcome Writer's Block	36
Plot Twists	40
Writing Prompts	47
Romance Writing Prompts	48
Sci-Fi Writing Prompts	50
Fantasy Writing Prompts	52

Teen Writing Prompts	54
Horror Writing Prompts	56
Supernatural Writing Prompts	58
Thriller Writing Prompts	60
Historical Writing Prompts	62
Mystery Writing Prompts	64
Superhero Writing Prompts	66
Futuristic Writing Prompts	68
Gothic Writing Prompts	70
Christian Writing Prompts	72
Crime Writing Prompts	74
Conclusion	76

What is Writer's Block?

It is that feeling when you sit down to write, and nothing comes out, or what comes out feels like rubbish. It is the bane of every writer's existence and can strike at any time, no matter how experienced you are. For some people, it is a fear of the blank page or a writer's anxiety. It can be caused by perfectionism or a lack of confidence. It might be procrastination or Indecision. It could be writer's block if you are struggling to come up with ideas, if you start writing and then delete everything, or if you just can't seem to get going.

There are many techniques, tools and advice from famous writers that can help you overcome writer's block, and this book will explore some of the most popular ones. With a little bit of effort, you'll be able to get your writing mojo back in no time!

Is Writer's Block Real?

Yes, writer's block is a real phenomenon. It is not just something people make up to explain why they cannot write. If you have ever experienced writer's block, you know how frustrating and debilitating it can be.

Quotes with Advice From Famous Writers

"The writer who experiences writer's block is not experiencing a failure of imagination, but a failure of will."

- William Golding

Advice from writer William Golding can be summarized as writer's block is not a lack of ideas, it is a lack of motivation.

"The cure for writer's block is not to write."

- Anne Lamott

This quote from writer Anne Lamott suggests that the best way to overcome writer's block is to take a break from writing. This could mean taking a walk, reading something else or just taking some time away from your work.

"I have long believed that the only real cure for writer's block is to stop being so damn self-conscious and pretentious about your writing."

- Stephen King

Famous author Stephen King believes that the best way to overcome writer's block is to stop taking your writing so seriously. This means not worrying about perfection or what other people will think of your work. Just write for the joy of it!

"The only way to get rid of my writer's block was to write more bad stories."

- Flannery O'Connor

Writer Flannery O'Connor suggests that the best way to overcome writer's block is to just keep writing, even if what you're producing is not your best work. This is an excellent way to get back into the flow of writing and to start generating new ideas.

"Remember: when people tell you something's wrong or doesn't work for them, they are almost always right. When they tell you exactly what they think is wrong and how to fix it, they are almost always wrong."

- Neil Gaiman

This quote from writer Neil Gaiman reminds us that it is important to listen to feedback from others, but not to take it too literally. It is helpful to consider other people's opinions, but ultimately you should trust your own instincts and go with what feels right for you and your story.

"The first draft is just you telling yourself the story."

- Terry Pratchett

This quote from writer Terry Pratchett reminds us that the first draft is not about perfection, it's about getting the story down on paper. Don't worry about making it perfect, just get it written!

"You can fix anything but a blank page."

- Nora Roberts

This quote from writer Nora Roberts highlights that once you have something written down, you can always go back and fix it. But if you don't have anything written, then there's nothing to fix! So the best way to overcome writer's block is to start writing.

"The writer must be willing to end up with much less than he started out with."

- Anton Chekhov

This quote from writer Anton Chekhov reminds us that the editing process is just as important as the writing process. Sometimes, in order to make a story better, you have to cut out entire sections or even characters. Be willing to make these tough decisions and your story will be all the better for it!

"Eliminate distractions, especially social media. Do whatever it takes to find uninterrupted time alone in a room."

- Unknown

This final piece of advice is anonymous but nonetheless important! To get the most out of your writing time, it is essential to eliminate distractions and create a space where you can focus solely on your work. This means putting away your phone, turning off the TV and finding a quiet place to write.

"Writer's block is a condition that affects amateurs and professionals alike. It occurs when we allow our fears to take over and prevent us from doing our best work."

- Steven Pressfield

This quote from writer Steven Pressfield highlights that writer's block can affect anyone, regardless of their experience level. It is caused by fear, which can be overcome with effort and determination.

"I have always believed that the right words will come to me when I need them. But sometimes they don't, and I end up having writer's block. In those situations, I just keep writing until the words come."

- J. K. Rowling

Writer J. K. Rowling suggests that sometimes the best way to overcome writer's block is simply to keep writing until the words come. This is an excellent way to get back into the flow of writing and start generating new ideas.

Summary Tips to End Writer's Block

- Get organized: This may seem like a no-brainer, but it's essential to have a clear plan before you start writing. Know what you want to say and how you want to say it. This will help your words flow more easily when you sit down to write.

- Take breaks: If you feel stuck, sometimes the best thing to do is take a break. Go for a walk, watch a movie, or read something unrelated to your project. This can help refresh your mind and give you some new ideas.

- Set a word goal: A specific word goal can help motivate you to keep writing even when you don't feel like it. Write 500 words, or even just 100. Once you reach your goal, you can take a break if necessary.

- Write in a different location: Sometimes all you need is a change of scenery. If you typically write at home, try going to a coffee shop or the library. This can help jumpstart your creativity.

- Talk to someone else: Talking to another writer can give you some great insights into how they overcome writer's block. You may even pick up some new techniques that you can use yourself.

- Take a writing class: If you're having trouble getting started, it may help to take a writing class. This can give you some structure and help you learn new ways to approach your work.

- Read other writers: Reading other writers can give you some great ideas for your own work. You may even find that you have more in common with them!

- Give yourself time: Don't expect to sit down and write a masterpiece right away. It takes time to overcome writer's block, so be patient with yourself. These tips will help, but it may still take some time before the words start flowing again.

Writing Techniques

We have collected several writing techniques that will help you get over writer's block and become a better writer.

- The Snowball Technique: This method involves taking a small action which then leads to another small action, and so on, until you have built up enough momentum to write a whole piece.

- The Dictation Method: This is where you speak your ideas out loud instead of trying to write them down. You can transcribe what you have said or even record yourself and play it back later.

- Write About Something Else: Sometimes the best way to get over writer's block is to simply write about something else entirely. This can help to take the pressure off and allow you to approach your project with fresh eyes.

- Write About Your Characters: Look into your character's souls and write about them and then work out where it goes later (when you are editing).

- Flip Your Chapter Upside Down: Try to change the order of events and see if you can get the chapter moving forward. Most of the time, this doesn't work, but when it does - it can really help.

- Take on a different perspective: Instead of writing from your own point of view, try taking on the perspective of someone else. This can be a character from your story or even a real person. This can help you see things in a new light and develop some fresh ideas.

- Write about something you're passionate about: If you're struggling to find something to write about, try choosing a topic you're passionate about. This can help you get excited about writing and make the process more enjoyable.

- Use prompts: If you're having trouble coming up with ideas, try using writing prompts. These can be found online or in books, giving you something to start with.

Once you get going, the ideas will start flowing on their own.

- Brainstorm with someone: Sometimes, it helps to brainstorm with someone else. This can be a friend, family member, or even another writer. Just talking about your ideas can help them take shape and come to life.

- Set a word goal: A specific word goal can help motivate you to keep writing even when you don't feel like it. Write 500 words, or even just 100. Once you reach your goal, you can take a break if necessary.

- Try a different format: If you're used to writing essays or articles, try something new, like poetry or fiction. This can help get your creative juices flowing and give you a fresh perspective on your work.

How Persistence in Writing Helps Overcome Writer's Block

Persistence may be the key to overcoming writer's block. In this chapter, we will discuss ways persistence can help you overcome writer's block and start writing again!

One way that persistence can help you overcome writer's block is by allowing you to find your inspiration.

A famous quote from William Faulkner says, "I only write when I am inspired. Fortunately, I am inspired at breakfast, lunch, and dinner."

This is a great perspective to have when you're struggling with writer's block. Just because you don't feel inspired at the moment doesn't mean that inspiration won't strike later. If you keep writing, eventually, the inspiration will come.

Another way that persistence can help you overcome writer's block is by allowing you to push through tough times. However, if you are persistent in your efforts, eventually, you will start seeing results. This will keep you motivated to continue writing and help you overcome any feelings of discouragement.

There will be times when writing is difficult, no matter how inspired you are. This is just a part of the process. But if you keep pushing through, you will make it to the other side.

So if you're feeling stuck, don't give up! Be persistent, and you will find your way out of writer's block.

How Lowering Your Expectations Helps Overcome Writer's Block

It can be easy to get discouraged when writing because you're not immediately producing the great American novel. However, it's important to remember that even the best writers had to start somewhere. Instead of getting bogged down by your expectations, try lowering them instead.

Just write down whatever comes into your head, and don't edit it until you have written the required word count. This will help you to focus on the process of writing and enjoy it, rather than worrying about the end result. Then you are allowed to go back and edit what you have written and delete or change sections once you know what direction your chapter is taking.

If you are part of a writer's circle and writing a new novel, imagine how you would feel if you spent weeks writing the first few chapters before asking for feedback on the book outline and characters, only to find that your writing colleagues hate them and suggest another plot altogether. It would be very disheartening, and you might feel like giving up.

Lowering your expectations can help prevent this type of situation because it allows you to get feedback early in the writing process before getting too attached to your work. This way, if someone does suggest a different direction for your story, you can easily make the changes without feeling like you have wasted all of your time.

So next time you sit down to write, remember to lower your expectations and just enjoy the process! Who knows, you might just surprise yourself with what you produce.

How Reading Books when Writing Helps Overcome Writer's Block

In this chapter, we will discuss some ways that reading can help you overcome writer's block and start writing again!

When you're feeling stuck, it can be helpful to take a break from writing and read something that will inspire you.

Reading can also help keep you motivated. It can be easy to give up on writing when you feel like you're not making any progress. However, if you are persistent in your efforts, eventually, you will start seeing results. This will keep you motivated to continue writing and help you overcome any feelings of discouragement.

If you are struggling with writer's block, reading may be the key to getting through it! By finding your inspiration and staying motivated, you can start writing again in no time!

How Brainstorming when Writing Helps Overcome Writer's Block

If you're feeling stuck, brainstorming can be a great way to overcome writer's block and get your creative juices flowing again.

To brainstorm, simply sit down with a piece of paper and write down whatever comes into your head. Don't worry about editing or making sense at this stage, just let your ideas flow freely. Once you have brainstormed for a while, you can start to organize your thoughts and see which ideas could work for your story.

Brainstorming is a great way to overcome writer's block because it helps you to generate new ideas that you might not have thought of otherwise. It also gets you thinking creatively, which can help jumpstart the writing process.

Brainstorming with a friend can also be helpful. This is because you can bounce ideas off of each other and come up with even more creative solutions. Plus, it's always more fun to brainstorm with someone else!

If you're feeling stuck, try brainstorming the next time you sit down to write.

How Stopping When You Are Ahead Helps Overcome Writer's Block

If you're feeling tired, stopping when you are ahead can help overcome writer's block and get you writing again.

When you stop while you are still ahead, you have done the required amount of work for the day and can stop there. This can be a great relief if you have struggled to write all day and feel like you need a break. It also allows you to return to your work with fresh eyes, which can help give you a new perspective on how to approach the rest of your story.

Ernest Hemingway famously said, "The best way is always to stop when you are going good and when you know what will happen next. If you do that every day...you will never be stuck. But if you get sick, it will be better for you if you stop before the illness gets worse."

So next time you feel stuck, try stopping while you are still ahead! This can help give you the break you need to return to your story with fresh eyes and new ideas.

How Having a Change of Scene Helps Overcome Writer's Block

When you're feeling stuck, it can be helpful to take a break from writing and do something that will inspire you. This could be reading your favorite book, taking a walk in nature, or listening to music. Once you have found your inspiration outside of writing, you can come back to your story with fresh eyes and new ideas.

A change of scene can help to break the monotony of staring at a blank page, and it can also help to stimulate your creativity. So if you're feeling stuck, try taking a break and doing something that will inspire you! This just might help you overcome writer's block and get your story moving again.

A famous writer who swears by this technique is Maya Angelou. Whenever she felt stuck, she would change her scenery and go for a walk. This helped her to clear her mind and find new ideas for her writing.

Maya Angelou is a world-renowned author, poet, activist, and speaker who has been recognized for her work on issues of race, class, and gender. She is best known for her autobiography I Know Why the Caged Bird Sings.

So, if you're feeling stuck, try changing your scenery and see if it helps you to overcome writer's block!

How Taking Regular Breaks Helps Overcome Writer's Block

What is the Pomodoro technique?

The Pomodoro technique is a time management strategy that can break down work into smaller, more manageable chunks. This technique is named after the Italian word for 'tomato', as the original creator of this technique, Francesco Cirillo, used a tomato-shaped kitchen timer to keep track of his work intervals.

The Pomodoro technique is based on the premise that if you break down your work into smaller intervals, it will be easier to focus and stay on task. Each work interval is followed by a short break, which allows you to take a breather and come back to your work with fresh eyes. You can buy tomato-shaped timers online to place in your work area.

The Pomodoro technique is a great way to structure your breaks. This technique involves working for 25 minutes and then taking a five-minute break. Once you've completed four work intervals, you can take a more extended break of 15-20 minutes. Taking regular breaks will help you to stay fresh and focused, and it can also help to prevent burnout.

A writer who swears by the Pomodoro technique is Leo Babauta. He is a best-selling author, blogger, and podcaster who has written several books on productivity, including The Power of Less and Zen Habits.

Taking regular breaks is an integral part of the Pomodoro technique. By taking short breaks between intervals of focused work, you can come back to your task with fresh eyes and renewed energy.

If you're struggling with writer's block, why not give the Pomodoro technique a try?

How Keeping a Writing Journal Helps Overcome Writer's Block

For many writers, the act of writing is therapeutic. It can be cathartic to get all of your thoughts and feelings down on paper (or screen). Sometimes, the act of writing itself is enough to help you overcome writer's block.

If you struggle to start or continue a story, try keeping a writing journal. This can be an ongoing document where you write down your thoughts and ideas, or it can be specific to a particular story or project.

Keeping a writing journal can be a helpful way to overcome writer's block. This therapeutic exercise can help to stimulate your creativity and get the wheels turning again. In addition, a journal can be a valuable resource to refer back to when you're feeling stuck. If you've been having trouble coming up with ideas, look at what you've already written and decide what you need to write to move forward. You may find that once you start writing, the ideas begin to flow, and you can finally continue with your story.

How Starting at the End Helps Overcome Writer's Block

When starting at the end, it means that the work is almost complete. You work out where the story will end and write your final and concluding sentence/s. This can help as a prompt to write the rest of the story, as you know what needs to happen for the ending to make sense. It also helps to create a sense of clarity, which can be helpful if you've been struggling with writer's block.

Of course, starting at the end isn't always possible or appropriate. But if you're stuck and having trouble getting started, it may be worth a try!

John Grisham says of his writing process, "I always start with the last sentence and work my way back to the beginning." By starting at the end, Grisham can create a clear roadmap for his story, which helps him write more efficiently.

So if you're struggling with writer's block, why not try starting at the end? It just might help you get your story moving again.

Does this chapter resonate with you? Starting at the end may not be possible or appropriate for every story, but it can be helpful if you're feeling stuck. If you're struggling with writer's block, John Grisham's approach may be worth a try!

How Using Software Helps Overcome Writer's Block

In today's world, it can be difficult to focus on one thing at a time. With so many distractions around us, it's easy to get sidetracked and push off our writing tasks until later. The good news is that there are tools out there that can help you generate ideas and produce the first draft quickly.

In this chapter, we will discuss the best software to beat writer's block and get your writing flowing again!

One of the most famous pieces of software for writers is Scrivener. This program helps you organize your thoughts and keep track of your progress as you write. It also includes several features that make it easier to start your writing project.

Another excellent option for writers struggling with writer's block is yWriter. This program is designed to help you plan out your story before you start writing. It includes features like a scene manager and a character database, which can help you keep track of your plot and characters.

WordHippo is an excellent resource for writers struggling with writer's block. This website provides many tools that can help you come up with ideas for your writing. It includes a thesaurus, which can help you find synonyms for words you're struggling to think of. It also has a word generator, which can create random words you can use in your writing.

Jasper AI is an artificial intelligence program that can help you with your writing. It includes features like a creative story template, a non-fiction writing recipe and 50+ templates to help you produce compelling writing. If you're struggling with writer's block, Jasper AI may be able to help you get a first draft done quickly. You could produce a draft chapter in 10 minutes. The free trial link https://jasper.ai?fpr=greenbubz includes a free trial with 10,000 words to test the software.

Plot generators are another great option for writers struggling with writer's block. These programs can help you create a basic outline for your story, giving you a starting point to work from. If you're having trouble coming up with ideas for your story, a plot generator may be able to help. The most popular one is Plotbot, which is free to use.

Character creators are another excellent tool for writers. These programs can help you create believable and interesting characters for your story. The most popular one is Character Builder, which is free to use.

There are a number of tools that can help you overcome writers block. Scrivener, yWriter, Jasper AI, and plot generators are all great options that can help you get your writing flowing again. So don't give up hope - there is software out there that can help you move past creative barriers to writing.

How Writing Exercises Help Overcome Writer's Block

If you're feeling stuck, sometimes the best thing to do is just start writing. It doesn't matter what you write – just get those words flowing again. Once you've started writing, you may find that the ideas begin to flow, and you can finally continue with your story.

There are several different writing exercises that can help to overcome writer's block. These can be as simple as setting a timer and writing for a certain amount of time or doing stream-of-consciousness writing, where you just write down whatever comes into your head.

Ethan Canin swears by a particular writing exercise that he calls "the main character dump." To do this, you simply write down everything you know about your story's main character – their appearance, their history, their personality traits, etc. This can help to jump-start your creativity and get you thinking about your story in a new way.

Richard Price tries a different approach, which he calls the "kitchen sink" method. This involves throwing everything and the kitchen sink into your story, even if it doesn't make sense. Price believes that by doing this, you can later go back and edit out the unnecessary parts. But in the meantime, it can help to get your creative juices flowing again.

Toni Morrison has a similar approach which she calls "overwriting." Morrison believes that it's better to write too much than not enough. She says, "If I can, overwriting is what gets the work done." By writing more than you need, you give yourself more material to work with later on.

Kurt Vonnegut takes an even more radical approach, which he calls "bleeding on the page." This involves writing until you literally can't write anymore. Vonnegut believes that by doing this, you'll be able to tap into your subconscious and come up with new ideas that you wouldn't have thought of otherwise.

Joyce Carol Oates also has an unusual approach to writer's block. She believes the best way to overcome it is to "write badly." Oates says, "I have always believed that the only way to get over your fear of writing badly is to write badly." By permitting yourself to write poorly, you'll be able to relax and let your creativity flow.

Elmore Leonard has a more practical approach to writer's block. He believes the best way to overcome it is to "keep your butt in the chair." He finds inspiration after reading the newspaper or taking a walk, but he always returns to his desk and continues writing.

E. Annie Proulx finds inspiration in visiting garage sales, where she often finds old books and objects that she can use in her stories. She also believes in the power of "immersion writing," which involves immersing yourself in your story's setting by researching or even visiting the location.

Isabel Allende tells why she always begins a new novel on January 8th, no matter what. She believes that by setting a specific date, she's more likely to sit down and start writing. Allende also believes in the power of rituals, and she has a number of them she does before beginning her writing day.

The CS Lewis exercise for writing vivid descriptions is to take an object and describe it in as much detail as possible. This can help to get your creative juices flowing and allow you to see your story in a new light.

The takeaway from these different approaches is that there's no one right way to overcome writer's block.

So there you have it – some of the different approaches writers take to overcoming writer's block. What works for one person may not work for another, so it's essential to find an approach that works for you. But if you're feeling stuck, these techniques may help you get unstuck and finally continue your story.

No matter your approach, the important thing is to keep writing. As Stephen King says, "The scariest moment is always just before you start." But once you get started, the ideas will begin to flow, and you'll be able to overcome that writer's block. So don't be afraid to put pen to paper and get those words flowing again.

Plot Twists

Plot twists help to add suspense, mystery, and intrigue to a story. They can also help to resolve plot points or move the story forward in unexpected ways. Plot twists can also be used to surprise readers and keep them guessing. We have included 65 for you to contemplate.

1. The protagonist discovers that they are actually the villain of the story.

2. The antagonist turns out to be the protagonist's long-lost relative.

3. It is revealed that the events of the story have been taking place in a dream.

4. The plot twist is that the story is actually a prequel to another story.

5. A character who was thought to be dead turns out to be alive.

6. It is revealed that two characters are actually the same person.

7. A major character is killed off unexpectedly.

8. A love triangle is resolved in an unexpected way.

9. A character's true identity is revealed.

10. The plot twist is that the story is set in an alternate universe.

11. A character turns out to be a spy.

12. It is revealed that a character has been lying about their past.

13. A character is revealed to have secretly been plotting against the protagonist the whole time.

14. It is revealed that a character is a robot or an alien.

15. A character turns out to have superpowers.

16. The plot twist is that the story is taking place in a post-apocalyptic world.

17. It is revealed that a character has been possessed by a demon or other supernatural entity.

18. A time travel plot twist is introduced.

19. It is revealed that a character has been leading a double life.

20. A character is revealed to be a murderer.

21. It is revealed that a character is pregnant.

22. A character is revealed to be gay or transgender.

23. A character has been suffering from a mental illness all along.

24. It is revealed that a character is actually an undercover policeman or detective.

25. The plot twist is that the story is set in the future.

26. It is revealed that a character has been kidnapped or being held captive against their will.

27. An evil twin or doppelganger plot twist is introduced.

28. A character turns out to be a witch, warlock, vampire, or werewolf

29. A character realizes they are in love with the wrong person.

30. It is revealed that a character is already married or in a relationship.

31. A character has to choose between two people they love.

32. One person in a couple is revealed to be cheating on the other.

33. A love triangle is resolved in an unexpected way.

34. A character declares their love for someone who does not reciprocate their feelings.

35. A couple gets unexpectedly pregnant.

36. The plot twist is that the detective is actually the murderer.

37. It is revealed that there are multiple murderers.

38. The plot twist is that the victim is still alive.

39. It is revealed that the murderer is someone close to the detective.

40. A major character is killed off unexpectedly.

41. The plot twist is that the story is actually a dream or nightmare.

42. It is revealed that the events of the story have been taking place in an alternate reality.

43. The plot twist is that the story is set in the future.

44. It is revealed that the murderer is a supernatural creature.

45. The plot twist is that the victim was killed for a specific reason.

46. The plot twist is that the murderer knows the detective.

47. The plot twist is that the detective has been working with the murderer.

48. It is revealed that the events of the story have been taking place in a dream.

49. It is revealed that the story is actually a prequel to another story.

50. A character who was thought to be dead turns out to be alive.

51. It is revealed that two characters are actually the same person.

52. A major character is killed off unexpectedly.

53. The plot twist is that the story is set in an alternate universe.

54. A character turns out to be a spy.

55. It is revealed that a character has been lying about their past.

61. It is revealed that a character is actually an undercover policeman or detective.

62. The plot twist is that the story is set in the future.

63. The plot twist is that the story is a prequel to another story.

64. It is revealed that a character is a descendant of a famous historical figure.

65. It is revealed that a character is the long-lost heir to a throne or fortune.

Writing Prompts

Writing prompts can provide structure and guidance for an author struggling to move forward with their story. They can also help to spark new ideas and inspire creativity. We have included 100+ writing prompts to help you get started, some of these are repeated across writing styles.

Romance Writing Prompts

1. A couple tries to keep their love alive despite being in a long-distance relationship.

2. One person falls in love with someone who is completely different from them.

3. A couple must deal with the fallout after one of them has an affair.

4. A relationship is tested when one person has to deal with a major life change, such as a job loss or illness.

5. One person is attracted to someone who is off-limits, such as a friend's spouse or a boss.

6. A couple has to deal with a difficult issue, such as infidelity or financial problems.

7. A relationship is challenged by outside forces, such as disapproving parents or exes.

8. A couple is trying to find their way back to each other after being separated by a war.

9. A couple faces the possibility of never being able to be together due to circumstances beyond their control.

10. One person begins to doubt their feelings for their partner.

Sci-Fi Writing Prompts

1. A group of people must find a way to survive after being stranded on a deserted planet.

2. An alien race invades Earth, and humanity must fight for survival.

3. A group of people discovers a new planet inhabited by hostile aliens.

4. A team of astronauts goes on a mission to explore a newly discovered planet.

5. A group of people are sent back in time and must prevent a disaster from occurring.

6. A group of people use time travel to fix things that have gone wrong in the past.

7. A group of people are caught in a battle between two warring alien races.

8. A team of scientists create a artificial intelligence that becomes sentient and begins to poses a threat to humanity.

9. A group of people are trapped in a virtual reality world and must find a way to escape.

10. A group of people must stop an evil corporation from taking over the world.

Fantasy Writing Prompts

1. A group of people must stop an evil sorcerer from taking over the kingdom.

2. A princess falls in love with a commoner and must choose between her heart and her duty.

3. A young woman discovers she has magical powers and must learn to control them.

4. A group of friends go on an adventure to find a lost city.

5. A wizard helps a young woman discover her true identity.

6. A dragon terrorises a kingdom, and a group of heroes must stop it.

7. An evil queen is trying to take over the world, and a group of heroes must stop her.

8. A group of friends must save their kingdom from an evil wizard.

9. A young woman discovers she is the heir to a kingdom she knew nothing about.

10. A group of friends must battle a group of villains to save the world.

Teen Writing Prompts

1. A group of friends must solve a mystery.

2. A group of friends go on an adventure.

3. One of the friends is different from the others, and they must learn to accept him/her.

4. The friends must deal with bullies.

5. One of the friends is going through a tough time, and the others must help him/her through it.

6. The friends make a new friend who turns out to be someone they never expected.

7. One of the friends gets lost, and the others must find him/her.

8. The friends have a falling out and must learn to forgive each other.

9. One person in a tight group of friends is moving away, and they must deal with the sadness and change.

10. The friends do something they know they shouldn't, and they must face the consequences.

Horror Writing Prompts

1. A group of friends are stranded in a haunted house.

2. A group of people are being stalked by a serial killer.

3. A family is terrorized by a demonic entity.

4. A group of people are caught in the middle of a zombie apocalypse.

5. A group of friends must deal with a curse that is bestowed upon them.

6. An evil spirit is possessing one of the members of a group of friends.

7. A group of people must deal with the aftermath of a nuclear war.

8. An alien race is abducting humans for experimentation.

9. The world is ending, and a group of people must find a way to survive.

10. A group of people must deal with the fact that they are slowly turning into monsters.

Supernatural Writing Prompts

1. A group of people must deal with the fact that they are slowly turning into vampires.

2. A group of people are being stalked by werewolves.

3. A family is haunted by ghosts.

4. A group of friends must deal with a curse that is bestowed upon them.

5. One of the members of a group of friends is possessed by a demon.

6. An evil witch is trying to take over the world.

7. A group of people must find a way to stop an apocalypse from happening.

8. A group of angels and demons are fighting for control of the world, and a group of humans must choose sides.

9. A group of people must deal with the fact that they have superhuman abilities.

10. A group of people are caught in the middle of a war between good and evil.

Thriller Writing Prompts

1. A group of people are being stalked by a serial killer.

2. A family is terrorized by a demonic entity.

3. A group of people are caught in the middle of woods in a log cabin, something or someone is hunting them.

4. A group of friends must deal with a curse that is bestowed upon them.

5. An evil spirit possesses one of the members of a group of friends.

6. A group of people must deal with the aftermath of a nuclear war.

7. An alien race is abducting humans for experimentation.

8. The world is ending, and a group of people must find a way to survive.

9. A group of friends must deal with the fact that they are dying one by one after witnessing a mysterious kidnapping.

10. A group of friends must deal with the fact that they are slowly turning into animals.

Historical Writing Prompts

1. A group of people are sent back in time, and they must prevent a disaster from occurring.

2. Write a letter based on the life events of one of your ancestors.

3. A group of people are stranded on a deserted island.

4. A group of people are caught in the middle of a war.

5. A group of people must find a way to stop an evil dictator from taking over the world.

6. A group of slaves must escape from a plantation.

7. A group of people must find a way to survive in the wilderness.

8. A group of people are stranded in the middle of a desert.

9. A group of people must find a way to stop a volcano from erupting.

10. A group of people must deal with the fact that they living the life of their ancestors.

Mystery Writing Prompts

1. A group of friends are investigating a series of murders.

2. A group of people are trying to solve a mystery that has haunted them for years.

3. A group of people are caught in the middle of a conspiracy.

4. A group of friends must deal with a curse that is bestowed upon them.

5. One of the members of a group of friends is possessed by a demon.

6. A group of people are being stalked by a serial killer.

7. A group of people must find a way to stop an apocalypse from happening.

8. An evil witch is trying to take over the world.

9. A group of people have been given superhuman abilities, and they must use them to save the world.

10. A group of people are stranded in a haunted house.

Superhero Writing Prompts

1. A group of people are given superhuman abilities, and they must use them to save the world.

2. A group of people are being hunted by villains with superhuman abilities.

3. A group of superheroes are fighting amongst themselves.

4. A group of people with superhuman abilities are trying to find a way to live normal lives.

5. A group of people are trying to find a way to stop an evil superhero from taking over the world.

6. A group of friends must deal with the fact that they have superhuman abilities.

7. A group of people are caught in the middle of a war between good and evil.

8. A group of friends must find a way to stop a machine that is going to destroy the world.

9 . A group of people are being hunted by superhero robots.

10. The world is threatened by an asteroid, and superheroes must find a way to stop it.

Futuristic Writing Prompts

1. A group of people are sent back in time, and they must prevent a disaster from occurring.

2. A group of people are caught in the middle of a chemical war.

3. A group of friends must find a way to stop an evil dictator from taking over the world.

4. A group of friends must stop a madman from destroying the world.

5. In the future, people can choose to have their memories erased.

6. In the future, a new form of energy is discovered that can be used to power everything.

7. In the future, a disease has wiped out most of the population.

8. In the future, the world is a utopia and everyone is happy.

9. In the future, the world is a dystopian nightmare and people are fighting to survive.

10. In the future, time travel has been invented and people can go back in time to change the past.

Gothic Writing Prompts

1. A group of friends must find a way to stop an evil spirit from haunting them.

2. A group of friends must find a way to stop a witch from cursing them.

3. A group of friends must stop a monster from terrorizing their town.

4. A group of friends are trapped in a haunted house.

5. A group of people are trapped in a medieval castle.

6. A group of friends must find a way to escape from a graveyard.

7. A group of friends are being stalked by a killer on Halloween.

8. A group of friends must find a way to stop an evil cult from sacrificing them.

9. A group of friends are stranded in the middle of a forest after a day hike.

10. A group of people are lost in a maze and they appear to go missing.

Christian Writing Prompts

1. A group of friends must find a way to stop an evil preacher from brainwashing their town.

2. A group of people are caught in the middle of a battle between Heaven and Hell.

3. A group of friends must stop an angel from falling to Earth.

4. A group of people are chosen to go on a quest to find a lost biblical city.

5. A group of friends must find a way to stop a demon from taking over the world.

6. In a small town, a relic is found and strange things start happening in the church. A child can communicate with a saint and starts to have dreams about the future.

7. In the future, a new Messiah is born.

8. The world is ending, and people are trying to escape to Heaven.

9. What would happen if Jesus came back to Earth.

10. In the future, the Antichrist takes over the world.

Crime Writing Prompts

1. A group of friends must find a way to stop a serial killer from terrorizing their town.

2. A group of detectives are trying to solve a string of murders.

3. A group of criminals are planning a heist.

4. A group of people are being blackmailed.

5. A group of people are being held hostage.

6. A murder has been committed and the group must solve it.

7. A group of people are caught in the middle of a gang war.

8. A group of people are trying to escape from prison.

9. A group of people are being hunted by the police.

10. A group of people are kidnapped and stranded in the middle of nowhere and they must find their way home.

Conclusion

There are many different approaches writers take to overcoming writer's block, but the important thing is to keep writing. As Stephen King says, "The scariest moment is always just before you start." But once you get started, the ideas will begin to flow, and you'll be able to overcome that writer's block. So don't be afraid to put pen to paper and get those words flowing again. I hope this book provided you with proven techniques and tools to blitz your writing deadlines!

www.ingramcontent.com/pod-product-compliance
Lightning Source LLC
Chambersburg PA
CBHW050321010526
44107CB00055B/2341